DATE DUE

ALL TIMES, ALL PEOPLES:

A WORLD HISTORY OF SLAVERY

OTHER BOOKS BY MILTON MELTZER

The Chinese Americans
The Human Rights Book
Never to Forget: The Jews of the Holocaust
Violins and Shovels: The WPA Arts Projects
Taking Root: Jewish Immigrants in America
World of Our Fathers: The Jews of Eastern Europe
Remember the Days: A Short History of the Jewish American

(with Bernard Cole)
The Eye of Conscience: Photographers and Social Change

OTHER BOOKS BY LEONARD EVERETT FISHER

Alphabet Art: Thirteen ABC's From Around the World
Letters From Italy
Leonard Everett Fisher's Liberty Book
Across the Sea From Galway
The Death of Evening Star
The Factories
The Hatters

ALL TIMES, ALL PEOPLES:

A WORLD HISTORY OF SLAVERY

MILTON MELTZER

illustrations by **LEONARD EVERETT FISHER**

Harper & Row, Publishers

ALL TIMES, ALL PEOPLES
Text copyright © 1980 by Milton Meltzer
Illustrations copyright © 1980 by Leonard Everett Fisher
All rights reserved. No part of this book may be
used or reproduced in any manner whatsoever without
written permission except in the case of brief quotations
embodied in critical articles and reviews. Printed in
the United States of America. For information address
Harper & Row, Publishers, Inc., 10 East 53rd Street,
New York, N.Y. 10022. Published simultaneously in
Canada by Fitzhenry & Whiteside Limited, Toronto.
FIRST EDITION

Library of Congress Cataloging in Publication Data
Meltzer, Milton, date
    All times, all peoples.

    SUMMARY: Examines the historical patterns
of slavery throughout the world, from ancient
times through the present.
    1. Slavery—History—Juvenile literature.
[1. Slavery—History] I. Fisher, Leonard
Everett. II. Title.
HT861.M43 1980   306′.3   79-2810
ISBN 0-06-024186-1
ISBN 0-06-024187-X lib. bdg.

Contents

1. Masters and Slaves

White, black, brown, yellow, red—no matter what your color, it's likely that someone in your family, way back, was once a slave.

For every corner of the earth has known slavery. And every people on the earth has been its victim.

The poor and the hungry, of course. But also the rich and the famous. Princes were made slaves, and so were millionaires. People were enslaved thousands of years ago, and people are still being enslaved today.

OPPOSITE: SLAVES FROM ALL OVER THE WORLD

A slave is a human being who is owned by another human being. For just as a person can own land, a house, an automobile, or a pair of shoes, so he or she can own a person. Like a horse, a slave can be bought, sold, hired out. A slave can be exchanged, given as a gift, inherited. How the slave feels about it doesn't matter. The master treats the slave as a *thing*, not as a person.

Imagine yourself as a slave. You have no rights. The law doesn't protect you. It is written to protect your master's power over you. You are his property, and the law says he can do almost anything he likes with you. What he most wants to do with you is force you to work. That is how he profits from owning you. You work as long and as hard as he wishes you to, at whatever job he wants done—and for nothing more than the food you need to stay alive.

A free man can stop working whenever he likes. Sometimes he does it at the risk of going hungry. But still, he can quit. He has a choice. You, the slave, can't quit. You are your master's tool, to be used whenever and however he likes, as he uses his plow, or his hammer, or his mule.

In your master's eye you have no will. He

decides everything. Not only the matter of work, but where you will live, what and how much you will eat, what clothes you will wear, when and how many hours you will sleep, whether you can have time for play or rest. Even whether you can marry, and the person you can marry. And if you have children, whether you can keep them with you, or whether they are to be sold away to some other master.

How such a life came to be is the story told here.

2. How Slavery Happened

Slavery started a long time ago, in the early history of humankind. It was not the invention of any one mind—few things are. It probably grew up in many places as the result of the same forces or conditions.

The earliest peoples got their food from hunting wild animals or gathering roots and berries. Either way, it was hard for them to feed themselves. There was nothing left over. That is why, when they raided other people, they killed them instead of taking them prisoner. If the winners had spared the lives of the losers, they would have been unable to feed them.

5

That changed as people learned to tame animals. The pigs, sheep, goats, cattle they raised were now their food. And as they learned to make tools—from simple choppers and axes to more specialized tools, such as knives, spears and fishhooks—people lived a little better. They made an enormous leap forward with the discovery of farming. Now people could produce more food than they needed. With their pots and baskets they could cook food and store it, and thus settle down in one place for a long time.

This easier and surer life made slavery possible. When farmers or shepherds could produce more food than they needed, they had an extra amount to feed the few people they might capture. Why kill defeated enemies when you could make them do your work at little real cost to yourself? When you could use them as you used other spoils of war? When you could, in a word, make slaves of them?

In this special sense, slavery was a step forward in the development of civilization. Losers in war kept their lives and in return were made to work. Slaves cared for the flocks and labored in the fields, making the master's life easier. The slaves in this way became new tools of production.

There is solid proof of how early it was that slavery developed. Archeologists digging into the soil of ancient buried cities of the Near East have unearthed thousands of clay tablets. Written on them are public and private records of all kinds. These letters, wills, contracts and law codes tell us that slavery goes back in history some 10,000 years.

In the old Near Eastern kingdoms of Sumer, Babylon, Assyria, people were divided into two basic classes: free people and slaves. At the top of society were princes, priests and soldiers. They lived off the food surplus produced by the farmers. Among the other free people were craftsmen, tradesmen and professionals. At the bottom were the slaves. Most of the slaves had been captured in wars fought with city-states nearby. The slaves were made to do useful work for their conquerors. In these small regions masters and slaves were from the same stock of people. They knew that if the war had gone the other way, their positions would have been reversed. Enslavement of the losers by the winners had nothing to do with race or color. In that sense masters and slaves were alike. Slavery was a question of plain power—of who had the strength to make others slaves.

To the south of these Near Eastern countries were other groups living in what we call the Middle East. There, on the rich soil of the Nile River valley, lived the people of Egypt. A somewhat different form of slavery took root in their land. Their rulers, called pharaohs, were considered divine or godlike, and therefore all-powerful. The pharaoh and his nobles, priests and officials lived off the great majority of the people, the peasants who worked the land.

Slaves, the prisoners of war, were not needed for basic labor because there were so many peasants. Those slaves who were fit for soldiering served in the army. But most of them worked in the palaces or on the temple estates. With the peasants they built the huge pyramids housing the tombs of the pharaohs. All the slaves belonged to the pharaoh; private citizens could not buy them.

When the Egyptian empire began to weaken, some small nations were able to thrive in the Middle East. The Hebrews, or Israelites, were among them. Around 4000 years ago a group of Hebrews, seeking to escape from drought and famine, moved to the Nile Delta and prospered. But later, when the Egyptians enslaved all the foreigners on their

EGYPTIAN OVERSEER

soil, the Hebrews were enslaved and made to toil in bondage for centuries. Finally, led by Moses, the Hebrew slaves made their escape from Egypt. After forty years of wandering in search of the Promised Land, they reached Canaan and founded what became the Hebrew kingdom.

Like all other peoples, the Hebrews, though once slaves themselves, made slaves of others. Most of their slaves were foreign prisoners of war. Some, however, were purchased from international slave traders. And still others were Hebrews sold into slavery by themselves or by others to settle debts. The slaves did work for the prosperous landowners, merchants and moneylenders.

Slavery for people who were not Hebrews was permanent. But in the case of Hebrews

HEBREW SLAVE

who had been enslaved for debt, the Bible offered the promise of freedom in the year of jubilee, which came every fifty years. "Proclaim liberty throughout all the land unto all the inhabitants thereof," says the passage in Leviticus. (Those words, much later, were engraved on the Liberty Bell that now hangs in Independence Hall, Philadelphia.) But how often the Hebrews obeyed this command is not known. Again and again the sages reminded the Hebrews that to free slaves was an act of great merit. The Bible also called on the Hebrews to shelter runaway slaves. The Hebrew law advised masters to treat their slaves like members of the family. The slaves were not looked down upon for being slaves. Slavery was considered an accident of fate that could happen to anyone.

China too, that vast land in the Far East, knew slavery. Ancient Chinese art showing field slaves working under the whip of overseers reminds us of scenes in Egypt of the same period. The first version of the Great Wall of China was built with slave labor.

Later, at about the time of Christ, a reformer called Wang Mang became the ruler of China. Many desperately poor peasants had sold their children or themselves into slavery, and other people, convicted of crimes, were sentenced to become slaves of the state. Wang tried to make the slaves' life less harsh and even banned the buying and selling of slaves. His ideas were resisted by the slave masters, and he was soon murdered. Over two centuries later, Chinese land barons had grabbed up so much land they had forced the small, free farmers into slavery.

Far more is known in the West about the slavery of another ancient people, the Greeks. In the early Greek culture of some 3000 years ago the people lived a simple farm life. Slavery was mild. Slaves were not treated like beasts of burden, but as human beings sharing the family system of labor.

But in the next several centuries the Greek world changed enormously. Greeks planted colonies all along the Mediterranean and Black Sea shorelines. As trade expanded and business flourished, new and independent city-states sprang up. Now the money that businessmen piled up became the measure of wealth. Using their money to make still more money, the prospering people bought slaves who produced textiles, pottery, armor and weapons, who built ships and dug tunnels and mined metals.

To get more and more slave labor, the Greeks turned to the old source, captives of war. At first Greek city-states raided one another and put their captives on the slave market. But the constant fighting created a demand for war materials, and as Greek citizens working in shops were drafted to fight, the labor supply shrank. So slaves were bought from many non-Greek lands. These countries sometimes sold their criminals abroad. Their poor people, burdened with debt, were sometimes sold into slavery in foreign lands. The slave trade boomed, with generals, admirals and pirates selling captured human stock to the dealers. Cimon, commander of a Greek fleet, put 20,000 prisoners on the slave market.

GREEK SLAVE MARKET

That was how it went in country after country, for thousands of years. It was always the same division of people—the free and the slave. And always wars were fought, prisoners taken and enslaved. Such wars have gone on endlessly. War itself became a "good business" because of profits from slavery. Two thousand years ago Roman generals seized whole populations of cities and sold the captives—sometimes as many as 50,000 or 150,000 at a time. Julius Caesar's troops took half a million slave captives during his campaign in Gaul (France). Rome grew rich on the slave trade that flowed across the Mediterranean.

Slave traders moved with the armies. In the town markets of the Roman world, the captive men and women were put up for sale like so many sheep. These slaves were from dozens of different cultures and of every color and creed. And they included children; enslaving children has been common throughout history. Children have been enslaved not only by capture in war; poor people in debt were often forced to sell their sons and daughters into slavery as well. Sometimes a father simply handed over a child to cancel a debt. In some places, such as Africa, helpless children caught alone were kidnapped and sold to slave traders.

ROMAN SOLDIER

13

3. From Africa to America

The black peoples of Africa knew slavery long before the white Europeans reached their continent. Like other peoples throughout the world, the Africans had practiced slavery since prehistoric times. They took prisoners in war and forced them into slavery, as they did their criminals. The trade routes that crisscrossed Africa supplied local markets with slaves as well as ivory, copper, silks and metalware. This trade was fed in part by the wars African kingdoms waged among themselves.

SPANISH
CONQUISTADOR

Before the Europeans came, African wars were usually local and small; they produced few captives. Slaves were used mostly within the household. In some kingdoms, however, slave workers were driven inhumanly, much as Africans would later be driven on plantations in North and South America.

It was Christopher Columbus who started the American slave trade. With his arrival in the New World in 1492, the building of colonies began. The European nations poured into the Americas to plunder them of their natural wealth. As they overran the Caribbean islands they forced the Indians into mining and farm labor. The Indians died quickly of the heavy work and the white man's diseases, to which they had no natural immunities.

Because the colonists were short of native manpower, they turned to Africa. Slaves could be bought on Africa's western coast. There the Portuguese had begun organized trading for slaves around 1450. At first the Arab chieftains of the southern Sahara had traded horses for slaves with the black rulers, selling these slaves in turn to the Portuguese. Then the English, French, Swedish, Dutch and Danish began competing for control of the African slave trade.

Meanwhile, colonists in the New World built up sugar, tobacco and cotton plantations. These required large-scale production and cheap labor in order to be profitable. And Africa became the source of that slave labor.

As the plantations spread in the Americas, they boosted the demand for slaves higher and higher. The African slave dealers adapted to the new need. African kings, rich men and leading merchants were eager to have Europe's manufactured goods. The hunger on both sides for slave trade profits led to a great rise in warfare. The coastal peoples of Africa bought or captured people from other tribes in the inland regions. These tribes in turn supplied themselves with people from still farther inland. Africans began selling slaves for guns, and using the guns to take still more slaves.

If it seems surprising that black men would serve as agents for the enslavement of blacks by whites, remember that whites have always enslaved whites. And in Africa, at that time, the differences between tribes were more important than race. Tribal Africans saw themselves as selling foreigners, people who were not their own people.

The men who brought the black slaves from Africa to the New World were a fantastic lot—

gentlemen and pirates, speculators and adventurers, seamen and surgeons. Like the planters who would buy their cargoes, the slave traders were tough, cruel and greedy. The English managed to beat out their rivals and take over more than half the slave trade.

These dealers in human beings were not looked down on. They did their profitable work blessed by church, government, monarchy and the public. Europe's kings appreciated the profits to be made and gave the trade their backing. (A favorite of Queen Elizabeth I, for instance, was Sir John Hawkins, the great English admiral and slaving captain.) Cargoes of wretched human beings were packed like sardines into wet and stinking ships' holds. There was enormous loss of life on the passage across the Atlantic. All told, some 10,000,000 Africans lived through the horror of the crossing to do slave labor in the Americas.

But even before the first African slaves arrived in the New World, there were slaves already at work there. Just as the Europeans found slavery when their ships touched African shores, they also found slavery among the Native Americans when they sailed along the coasts of North and South America.

For centuries the Aztecs of Central America had taken slaves by war or raiding, and made certain crimes punishable by enslavement. Among the Mayans of Central America a man could sell himself or his children into slavery. Along the northwestern coast of North America, from Alaska down to northern California, the Indians valued slaves as a mark of personal wealth or rank. The smaller tribes were constantly raided whenever stronger tribes wanted captives to sell as slaves.

Before the European settlers came, slave raiding was common too among the Indians in southwestern North America. And across the continent too, from Louisiana to Florida and up the Atlantic coast to Virginia, prisoners of war were made slaves for life. In the northeast, woodland tribes used slaves to make maple sugar, collect firewood and carry water. They worked in the fields and gardens, aided the hunters and served as paddlers and bearers to the native traders.

4. To Be a Slave

In every society, the rich and the powerful had the most slaves, of course. They owned scores of slaves, hundreds of slaves, thousands of slaves. And used them for every kind of labor imaginable, from the simplest domestic task of washing clothes to the hardest physical labor of mining or the most skillful brainwork of engineering. Odysseus, one of the ancient Greek leaders in the legendary war with the Trojans, was said to have 50 female slaves in his home. They did the household chores— washing, spinning, weaving, cooking and serving meals. Fifty may seem a lot, but later, in Rome, a single elegant family had as many as 400 domestic slaves. Still, that was little compared with Rome's richest men, such as Crassus. He owned 20,000 slaves, hiring out many of them to industry. The Roman emperors owned even more.

OPPOSITE: BABYLONIAN SLAVES BUILDING A TEMPLE GATE

GREEK SLAVE
MUSICIAN

The variety of work slaves have done down the centuries touches almost every occupation. Slaves have been hairdressers, doctors, tutors, farmers, librarians, philosophers, ranch hands, clerks, firemen, actors, musicians, gladiators, weavers, jewelers, carpenters, masons. On the huge plantations of ancient Rome as well as the vast estates of the West Indies, the American South and Latin America, mass labor has been required. Hundreds and often thousands of slaves have worked together to raise sugar, cotton, coffee, rice, tobacco, maize, cacao, for their masters. Slaves worked too on the big ranches, in the mines, in the shops, on the docks and in the homes.

Such labor requires strength and endurance. But other tasks assigned to slaves called for the complex work of the brain or the ingenious craft of the artist. The slaves of the ancient world—the Near East, Greece, Rome—designed and built palaces and temples for their conquerors, wove magnificent carpets and robes, worked metal into beautiful brass, gold and silver plate. In the Middle Ages the great manors used slaves alongside the serfs to do the work in the fields and in the households. The religious orders used slaves on their estates and in their monasteries.

On plantations in the Americas, the richer the planter, the more domestic slaves he used and the more specialized were their tasks. A wealthy planter's home would be full of cooks, butlers, waiters, footmen, coachmen, hostlers, laundresses, seamstresses, chambermaids and nursemaids. In the cities of the American South most of the domestic work was done by slave women. Men were used as valets, butlers, coachmen, stablemen, gardeners. Some slaves became expert brickmasons, carpenters and workers in iron. They built many a stately southern mansion and molded the beautiful iron grillwork of the gates and balconies of old New Orleans and Charleston.

SLAVE BLACKSMITH

Domestic work by slaves made for ease and comfort, but did not add to a master's wealth. Most masters in America tried to put their slaves to labor that brought in profits. They had their slaves work as mechanics and wagoners, build canals and railroads, man the tobacco factories and the iron works, the sugar refineries, the rice and flour mills, the cotton presses. Some masters hired out their slaves to other people, or let the slaves find such work for themselves. The slaves could then pay their masters fixed sums, and keep whatever they earned above that.

In the northern states slaveholding was less suited to the small family farms and to local manufacturing. It died out. New England shipowners, however, kept making money out of the slave trade. In the South the need for cheap labor on the large plantations made slavery profitable. It soon became the basis of the southern way of life. By 1860—just before the Civil War began—there were 4,000,000 slaves in the South.

What was it like to be an American slave in the nineteenth century? Most of the slaves lived in rural parts of the deep South. They raised cotton, tobacco, sugar, rice, hemp—the five great crops. Growing cotton was rough work. Women and children worked alongside the men in the fields. There was the plowing time, and then the many hoeings, and finally the cotton-picking season. Long hours—"from day clean to first dark"—with the overseer pushing hard, and the lash on your back if you fell behind. And when the fieldwork was done, you had to do your other chores: feed the mules, feed the hogs, cut the wood. Then at last to your cabin, worn out from the long day's toil. Now the fire to be made, the corn ground in the hand mill and supper prepared, as well as the midday meal to be eaten in the field tomorrow.

Children went into the fields at the age of five or six, toting water and helping alongside their mothers. Even infants spent whole days in the field, bound to the backs of their mothers. Boys and girls pulled weeds, cleaned the yard, hoed, wormed tobacco, or picked cotton. After the age of ten they usually had regular field tasks. Some slave children learned crafts and trades quite young. At eleven James Pennington was taught to be a blacksmith by another slave on his master's Maryland plantation. He took great pride in his skill and could make pistols, fancy hammers and sword canes.

As a boy in Baltimore Frederick Douglass,

AUCTION BLOCK

who became a great black leader, was assigned to run errands and to take care of his master's son, Tony, "to prevent his getting in the way of carriages and to keep him out of harm's way generally."

Families were often broken up by slave trading. Slaves in the American South were just as much for sale as the sugar and cotton they produced. Sale on the auction block was a routine business to masters, but a dreaded event to the slaves. They feared being sold on the block, because no matter how bad their life was, it could always be worse. Husbands were sold away from wives, and mothers and fathers were separated from their children. On May 2, 1849, J. T. Underwood placed this ad in the Louisville *Weekly Journal*:

> I wish to sell a Negro woman and four children. The woman is 22 years old, of good character, a good cook and washer. The children are very likely, from 6 years down to 1½. I will sell them together or separately to suit purchaser.

When he was about five, the slave Josiah Henson lived with his mother, brothers and sisters on a Maryland plantation. The estate was broken up and the slaves auctioned off.

His brothers and sisters were bid off as his mother watched, holding his hand. Then her turn came and she was sold. As Josiah was put on the auction block, his mother, half mad with grief, clung to the knees of the man who had bought her. She begged him to buy Josiah too, so she could keep at least one of her children. Refusing to listen, he struck and kicked her. "As she crawled away from the brutal man," Josiah recalled years later, "I heard her sob out, 'Oh, Lord Jesus, how long, how long shall I suffer this way?'"

Labor and life were harsh for the black
slaves of the South. But they struggled to make
a livable world for themselves and their children. The law viewed slaves as things, non-
human. Yet the slaves *were* human. They *did*
think and dream. They were imaginative

and inventive. They created their own family life, folk religion, music and art. They shaped ways to express themselves. They learned how to endure.

In this, American slaves were like the slaves in many other societies. They lived an in-between kind of life—treated as slaves, with no rights, yet sometimes shown affection. That in-betweenness must have caused the slaves both anguish and joy. Think of the slaves in ancient Greece. Athens, the leader of the Greek city-states, was called a democracy. She produced great poets, sculptors, states-men, historians, philosophers, perhaps be-cause this was the first extended period of free thought and free speech known to history.

But Athens' glory rested on a slave founda-tion. It was the largest slaveholding state of its time. Although every male citizen voted in Athens, the slaves could not. The condition of being slaves, said the law, made them unfit to be citizens. Yet it was the city-owned slaves who carried out the day-to-day duties of the government. They were policemen, registrars, accountants, scribes, heralds, executioners.

Like Athens, our own American democracy was birthed upon slavery. In 1776 the colonial leaders signed the Declaration of Indepen-

OPPOSITE: IN THE AMERICAN SOUTH

dence, which said, "All men are created equal." How deeply did they believe it? Were the slaves not human? Were they not entitled to "life, liberty, and the pursuit of happiness"? That question troubled many—like Thomas Jefferson and George Washington, themselves slave owners.

A troubled conscience is not easy to live with. But the slaveholders of that time found a way to ease their minds. In Europe as well as in America they developed an excuse for slavery: racism. As we have seen, slaves throughout human history might be of any color—white, black, brown, red, yellow. Up until about 300 years ago, there seems to have been no connection between race and slavery. But just about 300 years ago arose the mistaken belief that whites were superior to people of any other color, and that this superior race had the right to rule others. That racist belief—shared by many of the Founding Fathers—made it easy to justify the enslavement of blacks.

Jefferson and those American colonial planters who, like him, were troubled by the question of equality rarely took a stand against slavery or tried to change the slave system. Slavery was a crime, they felt, but somehow they could find no way to destroy it. They were not willing to give up their human property or lose political influence by actively opposing slavery.

So when independence was won from Britain, the Constitution of the new American democracy did not end slavery—in fact it prohibited Congress from *halting* the slave trade before 1808. The masters kept their slaves. For the sake of thinking well of themselves, slave owners would say they wanted their slaves, "their people," to be happy. But whatever they might do to make the slaves' lot a little better, they knew happiness could never arise from being a slave.

Throughout history and in all cultures, slaves learned to get some joy out of life, even under the worst conditions. They raised families, they worshipped together, they created songs and stories, they shaped beautiful things for the pleasure of themselves and others. In the American South, as the generations passed, they became deeply rooted in the land they tilled. They learned to use every means to secure more privileges from their masters and more breathing space for themselves. Always they struggled to assert their manhood and their womanhood. And sometimes they forcibly resisted their bonds, even at the cost of life.

5. "Troublemakers"

Slaves in all societies have always looked for ways to protect themselves from the cruelty of their condition. Some governments have even written laws to ease the slaves' lot. Four thousand years ago Babylonia had a code of law that encouraged slavery. But it also recognized that slaves were valuable. Masters were not allowed to kill their slaves. Slaves could be paid for some services. If they saved enough money, slaves could buy their own freedom. That narrow path to freedom was open in many societies, throughout history and down through American slavery.

OPPOSITE: ANCIENT TREADMILL POWERED BY SLAVES. SLOWING DOWN ON THE JOB WAS A COMMON WAY OF "MAKING TROUBLE" FOR THE MASTER.

But throughout history the vast majority of slaves could not earn the money to pay for their freedom. No wonder they were a "troublesome property" to their masters. Some ran away, some damaged tools and crops, some burned down buildings, some stole to keep from going hungry, some loafed on the job. Flight was the route to freedom taken by the Hebrews under their leader, Moses. They made their escape from Egypt and founded a new nation in Canaan. But a lone slave who ran away was much more common. If caught, he risked being shackled, mutilated or even killed. One old Roman boasted on his tombstone that he had hunted down 917 runaways and handed them back to their owners.

HEBREW EXODUS
FROM EGYPT

For American slaves, running away became almost the last hope of freedom. As the slave economy in the South flourished, the price of slaves rose. Masters were not likely to grant expensive slaves their freedom, nor could slaves any longer afford to buy it. By the middle of the nineteenth century the South's laws had made it almost impossible for a master to free his slaves even if he should wish it.

Flight became the only escape. Up creek beds, through swamps, and over hills the slaves headed to the now-free North in the dark of night. The network of routes they took was called the Underground Railroad. About 3000 black and white men and women served as "conductors" to help the slaves escape. The famous Harriet Tubman, herself a runaway slave, guided more than 300 fugitives to freedom on the Underground Railroad, earning the title "The Moses of Her People."

Thousands of slaves, usually the young people, fled every year. It was, like sabotage, a proof of how fiercely bondage was hated and

36

independence prized. Yet a Louisiana doctor said that flight was simply a peculiar illness. He called it "drapetomania—the disease causing slaves to run away." (Drapeto is a Greek root meaning running away; mania of course is insanity.) His "medicine" was to whip the devil out of restless slaves.

Every slave who got away was living proof to the others that they were not doomed to bondage until death. Freeing oneself was possible. But the slaveholders took great pains to prevent it. The plantations and the neighboring roads were policed. Patrollers with guns and bloodhounds tried to track down every runaway. The missing "property" was valuable, and its loss painful. Daily, the southern papers carried advertisements offering rewards for the return of runaways. Still, 75,000 slaves escaped to freedom in the fifty years before the Civil War ended slavery.

Suicide was the most desperate way of escaping unbearable slavery. There are records throughout history of slaves throwing themselves into rivers, leaping off roofs, stabbing themselves. One Roman slave choked himself on a sponge, another put his head between the spokes of a wheel. To such slaves, freedom in death was worth more than life in slavery.

SLAVE PATROL

37

6. Spartacus to Nat Turner

The masters' dreams were often troubled by the fear of murder or revolt. And with good reason. Some slaves tried to even scores by killing their masters. Sometimes they joined together to do it. A Roman master, Largius Macedo, was so cruel and haughty that his slaves surrounded him in the bath one day and beat him to death. A master out on a journey with his slaves might vanish forever. Slaves sometimes put poison in the food of a brutal master or mistress. The Roman custom was to put all a man's slaves to death if one of them murdered the master.

OPPOSITE: SLAVE UPRISING IN ANCIENT ROME

No master could feel safe, kind and generous as he might fancy himself to be. So masters spied on slaves all the time. In ancient Sparta they killed off slaves who showed talent for leadership. Still, Sparta's slaves rose up and it took seventeen years to crush the revolt. When Athens fought a long war with Sparta, some 20,000 slaves fled Athens to join Sparta. They were promised freedom, but many were sold back into slavery.

Slave revolts have continued to explode ever since. But not very often. Think of how hard it would be for slaves to rebel! It takes planning, organization, discipline, leadership. Under the tight control of slaveholders, how could you carry it off? But slaves did manage it somehow.

During the two centuries before Christ, slaves rebelled several times in the Roman Republic. The biggest uprisings were the three Servile Wars. The first took place on the island of Sicily. It was led by Eunus, a slave said to have the powers of a magician and a prophet. He began it with 400 city slaves; they then freed 6000 chained field slaves and armed them with axes, meat hooks, hatchets, slings, clubs, sickles and even cooks' spits. They were joined by a band of 5000 slaves from another part of Sicily, led by a herdsman, Cleon. The rebels won control of a large part of the island. When news of their revolt reached the mainland, still other slaves rose up there. The Romans, busy with a war in Spain, were slow to move. They found it hard to believe slaves could carry on a war so long and so well. For seven years the slave army beat off the Roman legions. Finally the slaves lost, betrayed by traitors, and 20,000 rebels were massacred.

A generation later slaves revolted in Sicily again. This time it took the Romans four years to put down the rebel army of 40,000. The third and last revolt, led by the slave Spartacus, set all Italy ablaze. It was the greatest slave uprising in history.

Spartacus was one of the many slaves the Romans trained to be gladiators. The gladiators fought in public to entertain the crowd. They battled in huge arenas where thousands watched them murder each other. Many gladiators hated their violent life. As professional fighters, however, they had the best chance for freedom. Spartacus plotted a revolt with 70 other gladiators in training in Capua, a town north of Naples. They stole knives from the kitchen of their training camp (their own weapons were always locked away) and fought their way out of the camp to freedom.

On the slopes of the volcano Mount Vesuvius, the rebels defeated the soldiers sent to capture them. This victory brought many other slaves to join Spartacus. Rapidly his force built up. The Roman soldiers, weakened by disease, cowardice and insubordination, fought poorly. Spartacus beat the Romans in battle after battle. When his army numbered 40,000 men, he began capturing towns. He showed the masters no mercy. He forced some to butcher one another in the arena, while the gladiators sat enjoying the spectacle.

But Spartacus knew his ragged army could never overthrow Rome's enormous power. His goal was to head north for the Alps. From the mountains the rebels could disperse to their own lands and live freely again. For two years the fighting went on. The Romans were furious at their failure to smash Spartacus, and sent eight legions to attack him. In the end his army was defeated. In revenge, Rome crucified 6000 slaves for daring to strike for freedom.

How Spartacus died, no one knows. But Rome and the world never forgot him.

Nor would the world ever forget another slave who led a great revolt—one that succeeded!—nearly 2000 years later. Toussaint L'Ouverture was born in Africa, captured in war and sold by slavers to a planter on the island of Haiti. Encouraged by his master, he read many books in history and politics. When his master made him steward of the estate, Toussaint showed great talent for leadership.

Haiti was a French sugar colony in the Caribbean Sea. Its slaves produced great wealth for the whites. Most Haitians were slaves, two thirds of them born in Africa. When Toussaint was a gray-headed man of forty-five, the French Revolution of 1789 broke out. Although the new French Republic proclaimed the Rights of Man, the slaves in Haiti were not included—in fact in 1790 the colonies were specifically excluded. The Haitian slaves revolted in 1791 and Toussaint became their black Spartacus. "Very small, ugly and ill-shaped," with "eyes like steel," Toussaint was a genius at organization. He trained an army of slaves to win victories. He forced France to abolish slavery in all its colonies. Now blacks were citizens too, equal to all others.

Toussaint set about creating a healthy society in Haiti, based on free labor. Under his leadership the former slaves won confidence and pride. They became legislators, diplomats, army officers, government leaders. Their Toussaint was now a great figure on the world stage. No longer was black skin a badge of shame.

But then Napoleon became dictator of France. He wanted to take Haiti back from the blacks and recover the great profits of its sugar cane. He sent an army of 20,000 veteran troops to the island. Haiti ran red with the blood of battle. When the killing failed, Napoleon tried trickery. He had Toussaint kidnapped and shipped to France, where he died in a mountain dungeon.

But Toussaint won after all. Napoleon gave up his costly attempt to force the Haitians back into slavery. The French got out, and shortly after, on the last day of 1803, Haiti proclaimed its independence.

In Brazil, during the 1600s, slaves saw their chance for freedom when their masters began fighting each other in a civil war. The slaves ran off from the towns and plantations into the thick forests. There they set up a government of their own, the Republic of Palmares, and built many towns. The whites invaded again and again, but were beaten off. Palmares lasted about seventy years. It went down to defeat only after a long and bitter struggle.

Revolt was tried in the United States too. There were many plots. None succeeded. One was led by Gabriel Prosser of Virginia, another in 1822 by Denmark Vesey of South

Carolina. Both failed, and the leaders were executed. A third broke out in Virginia in 1831. It terrified the whole country. Nat Turner, a slave carpenter, felt called by God to free his people and slay their oppressors. His small band of men roved the countryside for three days, killing fifty-eight whites and freeing slaves. As the alarm spread, local troops rushed in to put down the rebellion. Turner and sixteen of his followers were hanged.

Dead, Nat Turner became a legend. The whites trembled at his name. The blacks remembered him as a prophet who believed in freedom at all costs.

"That on the first day of January in the
"year of our Lord one thousand eight hundred
"and sixty-three, all persons held as slaves within
"any State, or designated part of a State, the people
"whereof shall then be in rebellion against the
"United States, shall be then, thenceforward and
"forever free; and the Executive Government of the
"United States, including the military and naval
"authority thereof, will recognize and maintain
"the freedom of such persons, and will do no act
"or acts to repress such persons, or any of them,
"in any efforts they may make for their actual
"freedom.

ABRAHAM LINCOLN, 1863

7. The Evil Must Go

It is a striking fact that during ancient times race and color had nothing to do with slavery. Slavery was universal and slaves were of every color. In the ancient world, among the peoples of the Near and Middle East, among the Greeks and Romans, color was not a dividing line. Whites enslaved whites by the millions. In China, masters and slaves were alike in color. So too among the Native Americans of the time before Columbus: Masters and slaves were of the same color. And again, in Africa before the arrival of the whites: Masters and slaves were of the same color.

So there was no racism involved in early slavery. Color was not the sign of bondage. Captured blacks and captured whites alike were enslaved, and no one debated whether the one race or the other was better suited to this condition. People realized that slavery rested on nothing but superior force.

Still, not even the great thinkers of ancient Greece ever thought of doing away with slavery. It was a fact of daily life that touched

49

OPPOSITE: Part of the Emancipation Proclamation, Which Freed United States Slaves

almost everyone in some way. The Greeks took it for granted. So did the Romans.

Only some of the ancient Hebrew brotherhoods, such as the Essenes, outlawed slavery in their communities. But then many centuries passed before voices of protest were raised again. In the eighteenth century a handful of Englishmen began to speak out, for pirates were capturing hundreds of British ships and enslaving their crews. Now that white Englishmen were the victims, some saw the evil of enslaving any human beings, including blacks.

But it was slow going. Many people profited hugely from slavery and the slave trade; they found it hard to act against their selfish interests. The antislavery movement grew slowly, and finally slavery was ended within Britain in 1772. It was later made unlawful for British subjects to engage in the slave trade anywhere. One by one other European nations banned the trade. Legally, slave trade across the Atlantic Ocean was soon dead. But that was only a paper victory. Outlaws of all nations carried on the trade in ships that sailed secretly from many ports.

The movement to abolish slavery spread from country to country. In America, the northern states banned slavery by the early

1800s. The number of freed black people grew. From their ranks came many leaders of the abolition movement. Frederick Douglass was the foremost. White abolitionists like William Lloyd Garrison, the Grimké sisters and John Brown joined them. They wrote, preached, lectured, organized, for the cause of black freedom. Often they met with bitter and violent opposition, in the North as well as the South. They turned to politics too, electing antislavery candidates to office.

Ever more men and women enlisted in the antislavery cause. But the peaceful efforts of the abolitionists were not enough. When Abraham Lincoln, who had pledged himself against the extension of slavery, took office as President in 1861, the southern slaveholding states tried to leave the Union. The Civil War began, with the North determined to preserve the Union. But the war rapidly developed into a war to crush slavery. The Emancipation Proclamation of January 1, 1863, was the turning point. And when the South was defeated, three amendments to the Constitution confirmed the battlefield decision. The Thirteenth Amendment abolished slavery; the Fourteenth protected blacks' rights as citizens and the Fifteenth their right to vote.

51

8. Slavery Today

While slavery in the United States died, in other parts of the world it lived on. The slave trade from East Africa to Arabia continued long after the Atlantic slave trade ended. Thousands of Arabs were busy in the trade, and some still are. In the 1880s one chieftain in the Sudan was using over 1000 slaves on his personal estate and 400 in his harem.

Slavery was still legal in a great many nations less than a generation ago. In China, Japan and Southeast Asia millions of children, some as young as four or five, were sold into slavery by their poor parents. Some worked as servants, many more in mines, small factories and stores.

OPPOSITE: NINETEENTH-CENTURY ARAB SLAVERS

In Africa, in the Arab lands, in parts of Latin America, there are still masters and slaves today. In Paraguay Indians of the forest are enslaved. In Morocco little girls of seven are enslaved in private workshops, making carpets. On the Aleutian islands off the coast of Alaska, the Indians have been forced to harvest fur seals under conditions of slavery. In Brazil thousands of people toil in forced labor on the rubber plantations of the Amazon jungle.

Forced labor is the modern form of slavery. In every former slave society, after emancipation the masters tried to find a substitute for slavery. Throughout the plantation areas of the world, after slavery was legally abolished, peonage or forced labor was introduced. Poor farmers going deeper and deeper into debt year after year were forced to work out what they owed. The law, written by the ex-masters, gave legal standing to this new form of slavery. And violence was used against anyone who objected. So though free in name, the ex-slaves were often, in reality, still enslaved.

In the American South, well into the early 1900s, white agricultural workers too were forced into peonage. Elsewhere, forced labor continues today in the form of "contracts" for paid labor, which become the means of pressing workers into almost unchecked slavery. Such workers wind up working endless hours for nothing, and never see home again. Guards, guns and barbed wire pen them in. They are sweated until death releases them from bondage. Peonage still goes on in many parts of Latin America. In Africa, where the Portuguese forced it on the blacks of their Angola colony, the "new" slavery ended only a few years ago when the Angolans won their independence.

SLAVE LABOR
IN SIBERIA

Forced labor is widely used today by totalitarian countries. These are governments of total domination. The state in these one-party systems is all-powerful and the citizens have no rights. In the first half of this century in the Soviet Union, millions of people were arrested on false charges and sent to prison camps to do all kinds of forced labor. Huge numbers died because of the terribly harsh conditions. Not until the death of the Soviet dictator Stalin in 1953 were many of the survivors released from the labor camps. During the Second World War, Hitler had 10,000,000 such slave laborers, taken prisoner throughout

Europe, grinding out their lives in his labor camps. The sick and the starving were forced to labor in German-owned rubber factories and coal mines. They were worked so hard that most died within a few months—to be replaced by a fresh delivery of slaves. The Russian Communists and the German Nazis introduced a system of mass slavery on a scale larger than anything known before.

Today the chief slave region extends across the Sahara Desert of Africa and into the Arabian peninsula. Though both law and the Muslim religion forbid it, slavery goes on. Children, bought from starving parents or kidnapped, are among the victims. Slaves in Arabia do all kinds of work. If they rebel, they are beaten or killed. Where lands are terribly poor, slavery is still accepted. Hunger binds the slave to his master.

So thousands of years after slavery was born, it continues to live. The labor camps of the brutal dictators create a world of the living dead. In places such as the islands of Indonesia, a military dictatorship, tens of thousands of political prisoners toil at forced labor. If you were unlucky enough to live in such a country, you might be one of the 10,000,000 slaves in today's world.

NAZI CONCENTRATION
CAMP VICTIM

9. And Tomorrow?

How can we get rid of slavery?

The United Nations, in its Universal Declaration of Human Rights, condemns it.

Yet little or nothing is done to stamp it out.

It is not hard to write good statements against slavery and get governments to sign them.

What is much harder to get is *action*.

Now and then the United Nations receives reports about slavery or forced labor in this country or that. The reports gather dust in the files. For as we have seen, slavery is deeply rooted in history, custom, tradition. Countries are reluctant to act against another country which may be accused of permitting slavery.

OPPOSITE: CAN THE UNITED NATIONS WORKING ALONE END SLAVERY?

Slavery gets little attention in the press. There are some private groups, such as the London-based Anti-Slavery Society and Amnesty International, which try to expose slavery and forced labor wherever they exist. But they do not have much political strength.

Slavery exists now in some underdeveloped parts of the world, in the poorer nations. There the people are hungry, ignorant, often without a voice in government. Nor do people have a voice in totalitarian countries, where forced labor may be the form of slavery.

Slavery could be abolished in all such places— if the governments would decide to do it.

To bring about such reform we must encourage, aid or shame governments into taking action. If the people in countries where slavery does not exist were to put pressure on such governments, it might help. If poorer nations were helped by the richer nations, that could make a difference too.

Slavery is an old, old example of a terrible urge human beings have—to dominate others. They do it for power, for pleasure, for profit. Unless governments adopt and enforce laws against slavery and its modern form, forced labor, the strong will continue to dominate the weak.

Suggested Reading

This book unfolds the story of slavery the world over. As it moves from slavery's beginnings in the ancient world to its practice in our time, it touches upon many fascinating characters and dramatic happenings. For those who want to know more about them, here is a list of books worth exploring. They help bring history alive, for they dig into the feelings and thoughts of people young and old who lived in slave societies, some of them thousands of years ago, others only yesterday. Through their experiences you will come to understand more fully the slaves' labors, their sufferings, their joys, their achievements, their spirit, their heroism.

Those titles also available in paperback are marked with an asterisk (*).

*Bacon, Martha S. *Sophia Scrooby Preserved.* Little, Brown & Co. (Atlantic Monthly Press), 1968. (Paperback edition: Dell Publishing Co., Inc., 1972.) The daughter of an African chieftain, sold into slavery, falls in with pirates.

Beyer, Audrey W. *Dark Venture.* Alfred A. Knopf, Inc., 1968. A twelve-year-old African boy, captured in tribal warfare, is shipped to New England, where he lives the life of a slave.

Bolliger, Max. *Joseph.* Translated by Marion Koenig. Delacorte Press, 1969. A retelling of the Old Testament story of Joseph, whose jealous brothers sold him into slavery in Egypt.

*Bontemps, Arna. *Black Thunder.* Beacon Press, Inc., 1968 (paperback). A novel based on the actual plot of Gabriel Prosser, a slave preacher, to attack Richmond, Virginia, with a thousand men and free the slaves.

Burchard, Peter. *Bimby.* Coward, McCann & Geoghegan, Inc., 1968. The story of a young slave on the Sea Islands of Georgia during the years just before the Civil War.

Collier, James Lincoln, and Collier, Christopher. *The Bloody Country.* Scholastic Book Services (Four Winds Press), 1976. A family living in the Wyoming Valley of Pennsylvania in the mid-eighteenth century is challenged by the striving for freedom of their half-black, half-Indian slave.

Dickinson, Peter. *The Dancing Bear.* Little, Brown & Co. (Atlantic Monthly Press), 1973. A Greek slave, his dancing bear, and an old holy man journey from Byzantium to the land of the Huns.

Dillon, Ellis. *The Shadow of Vesuvius.* Thomas Nelson, Inc., 1977. A Greek slave of a Roman artisan plans his escape from the city of Pompeii amid ominous signs of the approaching eruption of Mount Vesuvius.

Douglass, Frederick. *Life and Times of Frederick Douglass.* Edited by Barbara Ritchie. Thomas Y. Crowell Co., 1966. A giant among the abolitionists tells the story of his own childhood and youth under slavery, and of his unrelenting efforts to win freedom and equal rights for his people.

Edwards, Sally. *When the World's on Fire.* Coward, McCann & Geoghegan, Inc., 1972. During the American Revolution a nine-year-old slave girl is given the task of blowing up the ammunition stores in the British barracks in Charleston.

Forman, James. *So Ends This Day.* Farrar, Straus & Giroux, Inc., 1970. In the 1840s, Guy and Bonnie go on a long voyage on their father's whaler, pursuing the slave ship captained by their mother's murderer.

*Fox, Paula. *The Slave Dancer.* Bradbury Press, 1973. (Paperback edition: Dell Publishing Co., Inc., 1975.) A thirteen-year-old boy, kidnapped by the crew of an Africa-bound ship, discovers that he is on a slaver and his job is to play music for the exercise periods of the human cargo.

Haugaard, Erik C. *A Slave's Tale.* Houghton Mifflin Co., 1965. Helga, a slave girl of old Norway, stows away on a Viking ship when it sails for Brittany.

Haynes, Betsy. *Cowslip.* Thomas Nelson, Inc., 1973. The troubles of a thirteen-year-old slave girl in the beginning of the Civil War.

*Lester, Julius, ed. *To Be a Slave.* The Dial Press, 1968. (Paperback edition: Dell Publishing Co., Inc., 1975.) A chronicle of tragedy assembled from the eloquent slaves themselves, accompanied by editorial commentary.

*Meltzer, Milton, ed. *In Their Own Words: A History of the American Negro, 1619–1865.* Thomas Y. Crowell Co., 1964. (Paperback edition: Harper & Row, Publishers, Apollo Editions.) A first-hand account by American blacks of their life in slave times, taken from contemporary letters, diaries, speeches, journals, newspapers.

*Meltzer, Milton. *Underground Man.* Bradbury Press, 1972. (Paperback edition: Dell Publishing Co., Inc., 1974.) Josh, a courageous young white, lives "underground" in the South, helping slaves to escape to freedom. Betrayed and captured, he finds out what prison life is like.

Ortiz, Victoria. *Sojourner Truth.* J. B. Lippincott Co., 1974. How a frightened, lonely slave child found her courage and her freedom, and the strength to help free others.

Ray, Mary. *The Eastern Beacon.* Farrar, Straus & Giroux, Inc., 1966. In A.D. 296, a boy and girl are washed ashore on one of the Scilly Isles off England's coast, where they are captured by a hostile people and forced into slavery.

Ray, Mary. *The Ides of April.* Farrar, Straus & Giroux, Inc., 1975. When a Roman senator is murdered in the time of Nero, his slaves are all imprisoned, but young Hylas escapes and tries to find the real killer to save his friends from execution.

Rossman, Parker. *Pirate Slave.* Thomas Nelson, Inc., 1976. A twelve-year-old boy in the early nineteenth century is captured by Muslim pirates and forced into a life of slave trading off the North African coast.

Scott, John Anthony. *Hard Trials on My Way: Slavery and the Struggle Against It.* Alfred A. Knopf, Inc., 1974. A rounded picture of life in the slave South and of the struggle for emancipation.

Sterling, Dorothy. *Freedom Train: The Story of Harriet Tubman.* Doubleday & Co., Inc., 1964. The adventures of the remarkable woman who ran away to freedom and returned south many times to rescue hundreds of other slaves.

Sterling, Dorothy, ed. *The Trouble They Seen: Black People Tell the Story of Reconstruction.* Doubleday & Co., Inc., 1976. A dramatic reconstruction of the post-Civil War period as seen by free blacks whose aspirations were drowned in a southern reign of terror, foreshadowing the Black Power movement a century later.

*Sterne, Emma G. *The Long Black Schooner.* Follett Publishing Co., 1965. (Paperback edition, entitled *Slave Ship*: Scholastic Book Services, 1973.) How black captives aboard the slave ship *Amistad* seized control of the vessel, were tricked into landing it on Long Island, but finally gained their freedom through a struggle in the courts.

Sutcliff, Rosemary. *Blood Feud.* E. P. Dutton & Co., Inc., 1977. Sold into slavery to the Northmen in the tenth century, a young Englishman becomes involved in a blood feud that leads him across the Baltic Sea through Russia down into Constantinople and a different way of life.

Syme, Ronald. *Toussaint, the Black Liberator.* William Morrow & Co., Inc., 1971. How a slave coachman organized the blacks of Haiti and led them to a victorious revolt against their French masters.

Trevino, Elizabeth Borton de. *I, Juan de Pareja.* Farrar, Straus & Giroux, Inc., 1965. Juan, the black slave and assistant to the Spanish painter Velazquez, tells of his life with the artist.

Vining, Elizabeth Gray. *The Taken Girl.* The Viking Press, Inc., 1972. An orphan girl taken on as a helper in the Quaker household of the poet John Greenleaf Whittier becomes caught up in the antislavery movement.

White, Anne Terry. *Human Cargo: The Story of the Atlantic Slave Trade.* Garrard Publishing Co. (1977?). Torn from their African homelands, millions of men, women, and children were carried across the Atlantic and sold into slavery in the Americas.

Index

64

65

MILTON MELTZER is widely known for his books on history, biography, and social reform. *In Their Own Words*, a documentary history of black Americans, won the Thomas Alva Edison Award. *A Pictorial History of Black Americans*, written with Langston Hughes, and *Slavery* are two of his most popular histories. His biography *Langston Hughes* was nominated for the National Book Award, as were three of his books about the Jewish experience: *Remember the Days*; *World of Our Fathers*; and *Never to Forget: The Jews of the Holocaust. Brother, Can You Spare a Dime?*, about the Great Depression, won the Christopher Award. Mr. Meltzer has also written three biographies of major antislavery figures. Currently he holds an adjunct professorship of history at the University of Massachusetts, for which he is editing the letters of the abolitionist Lydia Maria Child.

Born in Worcester, Massachusetts, Mr. Meltzer was educated at Columbia University. He and his wife, Hilda, live in New York City. They have two daughters.

LEONARD EVERETT FISHER has illustrated some 200 books for young readers, 35 of which he also wrote. Mr. Fisher is the recipient of a Pulitzer Art Scholarship, Italy's *Premio Grafico* prize at the 5th International Book Fair in Bologna, the Medallion of the University of Southern Mississippi for "distinguished contributions to children's literature," as well as citations from the American Institute of Graphic Arts, the American Library Association, and the National Council of Social Studies. He has designed ten U.S. postage stamps, and serigraphs of his art were used in a mural for the Washington Monument.

Mr. Fisher was born in New York City and was graduated from Yale University School of Art. He is Professor of Fine Arts and Dean of Academic Affairs at the Paier School of Art in Hamden, Connecticut, and a frequent lecturer at schools and universities throughout America. He and his wife, Margery, live in Westport, Connecticut. They have three children.